Listening to Leaders

Why Should I Listen to MY DOCTOR?

Christine Honders

PowerKiDS press™

NEW YORK

Published in 2020 by The Rosen Publishing Group, Inc.
29 East 21st Street, New York, NY 10010

Editor: Greg Roza
Book Design: Rachel Rising

Photo Credits: Cover, p. 13 michaeljung/Shutterstock.com; Cover (background) Rob Byron/Shutterstock.com; p. 5 George Rudy/Shutterstock.com; p. 7 Blend Images/Shutterstock.com; p. 9 sirtravelalot/Shutterstock.com; p. 11 Terry Vine/Blend Images/Getty Images; p. 15 ESB Professional/Shutterstock.com; p. 17 Science Photo Library - IAN HOOTON./Brand X Pictures/Getty Images; 19 Monkey Business Images/Shutterstock.com; p. 21 GagliardiImages/Shutterstock.com; p. 22 kurhan/Shutterstock.com.

Cataloging-in-Publication Data

Names: Honders, Christine.
Title: Why should I listen to my doctor? / Christine Honders.
Description: New York : PowerKids Press, 2020. | Series: Listening to leaders
Identifiers: ISBN 9781538341605 (pbk.) | ISBN 9781538341629 (library bound) | ISBN 9781538341612 (6 pack)
Subjects: LCSH: Children--Medical examinations--Juvenile literature. | Medical care--Juvenile literature. | Physicians--Juvenile literature.
Classification: LCC RJ50.5 H66 2019 | DDC 618.92'0075--dc23

Manufactured in the United States of America

CPSIA Compliance Information: Batch #CSPK19 For further information contact Rosen Publishing, New York, New York at 1-800-237-9932.

Contents

Health Experts

You wake up one morning and your throat is so sore that you can't swallow. You feel hot and your head hurts. Your parents decide to take you to a doctor. Doctors are people who are trained to figure out what makes people sick and how to make them better.

But I'm Not Sick!

Sometimes we go to the doctor when we aren't sick. It's a good idea for kids to see a doctor once a year. Doctors want to make sure that you're growing properly. They also want to teach you how to keep your body safe and healthy.

Checkups

Sometimes checkups are called "well-visits" because you go once a year even if you feel fine. During the visit, the nurse starts by checking your weight and height. He or she checks your blood pressure, which makes sure your heart is pumping enough blood around your body. The nurse also checks your temperature.

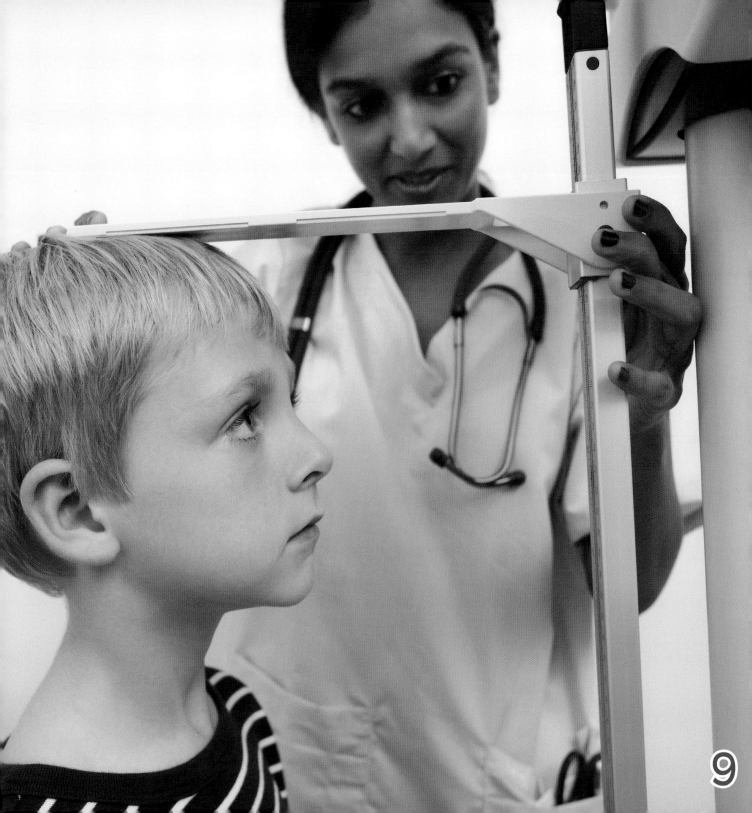

9

What Doctors Do

Doctors are like detectives. They look at your **symptoms** and ask you questions. They may give you tests for different parts of your body. They put the pieces together like a puzzle to figure out your **illness**. Then, they tell you what to do to feel better.

Different Kinds of Doctors

Pediatricians are trained to take care of kids. Some doctors only take care of elderly adults. Some doctors are specialists. That means they deal with certain body parts, such as bones, the heart, or the skin. Some doctors are experts in helping women have babies. Other doctors work in emergency rooms.

The Doctor's Exam

When the doctor comes in, he or she will ask you questions about how you feel. Then, the doctor listens to your heart and lungs with a **stethoscope**. The doctor also looks into your ears, eyes, nose, and throat with a special light. These tools help doctors see if something inside your body doesn't look or sound right.

The doctor looks at your backbone to make sure it's growing nice and straight. Then, you'll lie down on the exam table. The doctor then pushes on your belly to make sure your stomach and other **organs** are healthy. Doctors can tell if something is wrong just by feeling around.

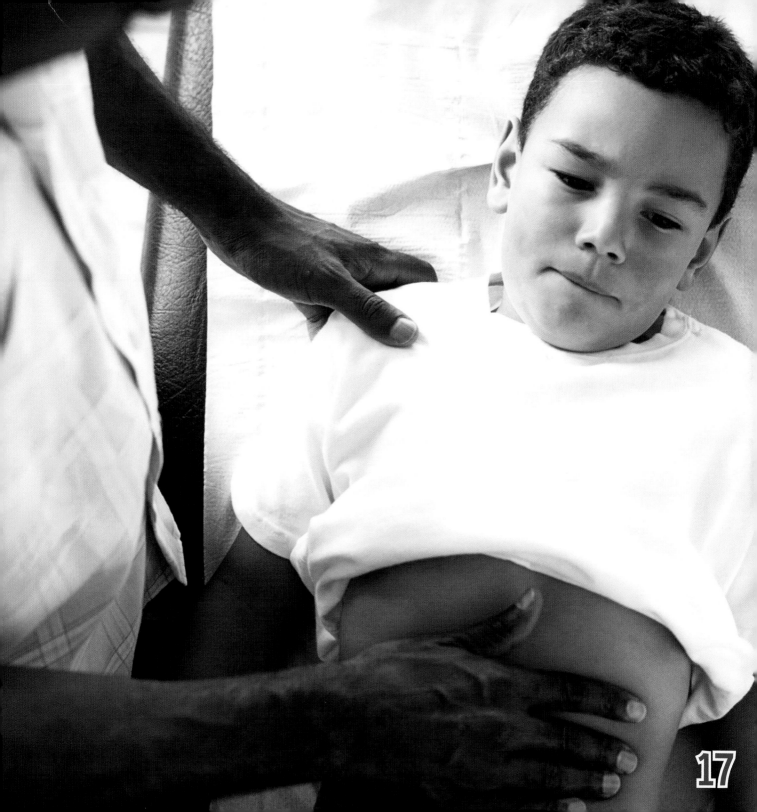

Questions and Answers

At the end of the checkup you may have questions. Don't be too shy to ask. Doctors are health experts and want to help you. If the doctor finds something wrong, he or she will tell you what to do to get better. If the doctor gives you medicine, take it when you're supposed to.

An Apple a Day

At the end of the visit, the doctor will talk to you about your health and safety. The doctor will remind you to wear bike helmets and sunscreen during the summer. He or she will explain how important it is to get daily exercise. The doctor will also teach you about good **nutrition** and what kinds of food to **avoid**.

Follow the Doctor's Orders

Doctors go to school for years to learn how to take care of people. They know how to keep you healthy and what to do when you are sick. That's why it's important to follow the doctor's orders. If you listen to your doctor, you will have a happy, healthy life!

Glossary

avoid: To stay away from.

illness: Sickness.

nutrition: The processes by which a living thing takes in and uses vitamins, minerals, and other nutrients.

organ: A part of the body that has a certain job.

pediatrician: A doctor trained to treat kids and babies.

stethoscope: A tool that lets doctors hear sounds inside the body, such as a heartbeat or breathing.

symptoms: Changes in the body that are signs of a sickness.

Index

C
checkups, 8, 18

H
heart, 8, 12, 14

I
illness, 10

M
medicine, 18

N
nurse, 8
nutrition, 20

O
organs, 16

P
pediatricians, 12

S
specialists, 12
stethoscope, 14
symptoms, 10

T
temperature, 8
tools, 14

Websites

Due to the changing nature of Internet links, PowerKids Press has developed an online list of websites related to the subject of this book. This site is updated regularly. Please use this link to access the list: www.powerkidslinks.com/ltl/doctor